★ The ★
UNITED
STATES
PRESIDENTS

Gerald

FORD

Megan M. Gunderson

Big Buddy Books
An Imprint of Abdo Publishing
abdopublishing.com

abdopublishing.com

Published by Abdo Publishing, a division of ABDO, PO Box 398166, Minneapolis, Minnesota 55439.
Copyright © 2017 by Abdo Consulting Group, Inc. International copyrights reserved in all countries. No
part of this book may be reproduced in any form without written permission from the publisher. Big Buddy
Books™ is a trademark and logo of Abdo Publishing.

Printed in the United States of America, North Mankato, Minnesota
062016
092016

THIS BOOK CONTAINS
RECYCLED MATERIALS

Design: Sarah DeYoung, Mighty Media, Inc.
Production: Mighty Media, Inc.
Editor: Paige Polinsky
Cover Photograph: Getty Images
Interior Photographs: AP Images (pp. 19, 21); Corbis (pp. 5, 7, 17); Ford Library (pp. 6, 9, 11, 13, 15, 25);
    Getty Images (pp. 7, 23, 27, 29)

Cataloging-in-Publication Data

Names: Gunderson, Megan M., author.
Title: Gerald Ford / by Megan M. Gunderson.
Description: Minneapolis, MN : Abdo Publishing, [2017] | Series: United States
    presidents | Includes bibliographical references and index.
Identifiers: LCCN 2015957284 | ISBN 9781680780932 (lib. bdg.) |
    ISBN 9781680775136 (ebook)
Subjects: LCSH: Ford, Gerald, 1913-2006--Juvenile literature. | Presidents--
    United States--Biography--Juvenile literature. | United States--Politics and
    government--1974-1977--Juvenile literature.
Classification: DDC 973.925/092 [B]--dc23
LC record available at http://lccn.loc.gov/2015957284

Contents

Gerald Ford

Gerald Ford was the thirty-eighth US president. As a young man, Ford worked as a **lawyer**. He also fought in the US Navy during **World War II**. Later, Ford joined the US House of **Representatives**.

In 1973, Vice President Spiro T. Agnew **resigned**. President Richard Nixon chose Ford to replace Agnew. But a **scandal** soon forced Nixon to resign too. So in 1974, Ford became president. Ford improved the **economy** and brought trust back to the American presidency.

Timeline

1913
On July 14, Gerald Rudolph Ford Jr. was born in Omaha, Nebraska.

1948
Ford was elected to the US House of **Representatives**.

1941
Ford **graduated** from Yale Law School.

1942
Ford joined the US Navy.

1974

President Richard
Nixon **resigned**.
Ford became
the thirty-eighth
US president on
August 9.

1999

Ford received
the Presidential
Medal of
Freedom.

1973

On December 6,
Ford replaced
Spiro T. Agnew
as vice president.

2006

On December 26,
Gerald Ford died.

7

Young Gerald

Gerald Rudolph Ford Jr. was born on July 14, 1913, in Omaha, Nebraska. His parents, Dorothy and Leslie King, named him Leslie King Jr. They **divorced** days later.

Dorothy and her son moved to Grand Rapids, Michigan. She soon married Gerald Ford. He renamed her son Gerald Ford Jr.

★ FAST FACTS ★

Born: July 14, 1913

Wife: Elizabeth Anne "Betty" Bloomer (1918–2011)

Children: four

Political Party: Republican

Age at Inauguration: 61

Years Served: 1974–1977

Vice President: Nelson A. Rockefeller

Died: December 26, 2006, age 93

Gerald Jr. was often called Jerry for short. His mother also called him Junie.

Football Star

Gerald **graduated** from Grand Rapids South High School in 1931. He then began attending the University of Michigan in Ann Arbor. He played on the school's football team.

At Michigan, Gerald studied **economics** and **political** science. He also served in student government. Gerald graduated in 1935.

Two major football teams tried to hire Gerald to play for them after graduation. But he turned both down. Instead, Gerald chose to coach sports and become a **lawyer**.

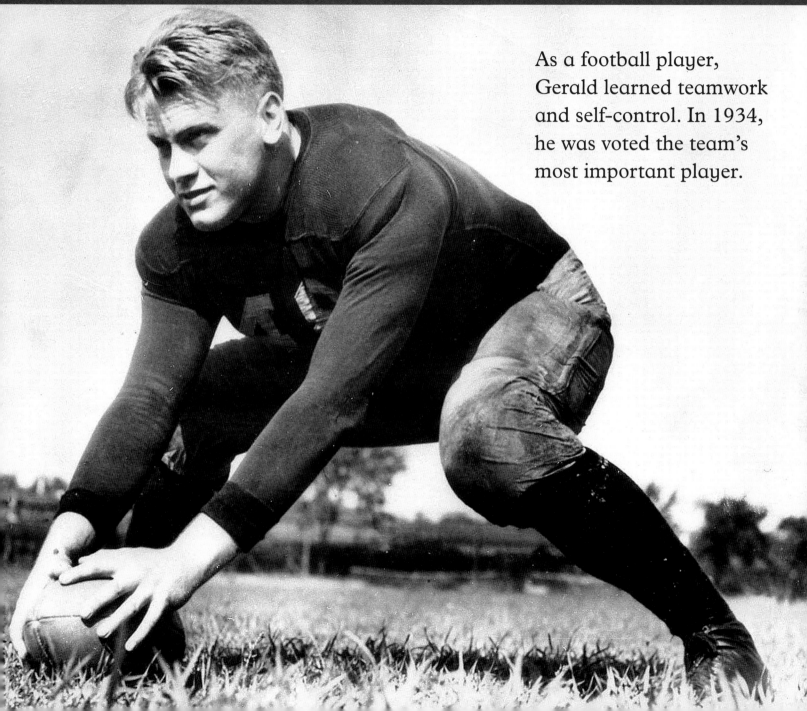

As a football player, Gerald learned teamwork and self-control. In 1934, he was voted the team's most important player.

Law and War

Soon after **graduation**, Ford began working at Yale University in New Haven, Connecticut. He coached football and boxing. In 1938, he began attending Yale Law School.

Ford finished law school in 1941. He then returned to Grand Rapids. There, Ford opened a law office with a friend.

In 1942, Ford joined the US Navy. He fought in **World War II** and became a **lieutenant** commander. In 1946, he returned to Michigan. There, Ford began considering **politics**.

In the navy, Ford served as an assistant officer aboard the USS *Monterey*.

Politics and Family

On June 17, 1948, Ford announced his decision to run for the US House of **Representatives**. He spoke well during the campaign. He also listened to voters' concerns. Ford easily won the election in November.

Meanwhile, on October 15, 1948, Ford had married Elizabeth Anne "Betty" Bloomer. Together they had four children. Michael was born in 1950. John followed in 1952. Then, in 1956, Steven was born. The Fords welcomed their daughter, Susan, in 1957.

The Ford family (*left to right*): Michael, Michael's wife, President Ford, the First Lady, John, Susan, and Steven

Congressman Ford

As Congressman, Ford listened to voters. He also worked with those who opposed him. He became known as hardworking and honest.

Michigan voters liked Ford. They reelected him 12 times! From 1951 to 1965, Ford helped direct government spending as a congressman.

On November 22, 1963, President John F. Kennedy was **assassinated**. Ford was appointed to the Warren **Commission**. The commission members studied the murder. They decided that the killer had acted alone.

In 1965, Ford (*left*) cowrote a book about the Warren Commission's decision. It is called *Portrait of the Assassin*.

While in Congress, Ford voted for two very important bills. The **Civil Rights** Act passed in 1964. It made unequal treatment based on race illegal. In 1965, the Voting Rights Act passed. It helped African Americans vote.

That year, Ford became the new House **minority leader**. He traveled the country to aid other **Republicans**. Ford served for another eight years. Eventually, he decided that the 1974 election would be his last. Yet his plans were about to change.

> ★ DID YOU KNOW? ★
>
> In 1974, Ford became the first president to visit Japan while in office.

Richard Nixon (*left*) welcomed Ford to Congress. The two future presidents soon became friends.

Appointed Leader

In 1973, Vice President Spiro T. Agnew was charged with trading favors for money. He **resigned** in October. Now, President Richard Nixon needed a new vice president. Nixon and his advisers felt Ford was the best choice. Ford won **support** from the House and the Senate.

Gerald Ford became vice president on December 6, 1973. It was the first time a US vice president had not been elected by the people. Ford traveled across the country supporting the **Republican** Party.

Spiro T. Agnew (*pictured*) was the second vice president in US history to resign. The first was John C. Calhoun in 1832.

Meanwhile, a new **scandal** was revealed. In 1972, burglars had broken into the Watergate building in Washington, DC. There, **Republicans** had tried to steal secret **Democratic** Party information. The White House hid its connection to the scandal.

President Nixon tried and failed to clear his name. On August 8, 1974, he **resigned**. The next day, Ford became the thirty-eighth US president. He asked Americans to move forward.

On September 8, President Ford **pardoned** Nixon for the Watergate scandal. This angered many Americans. Ford's popularity quickly dropped.

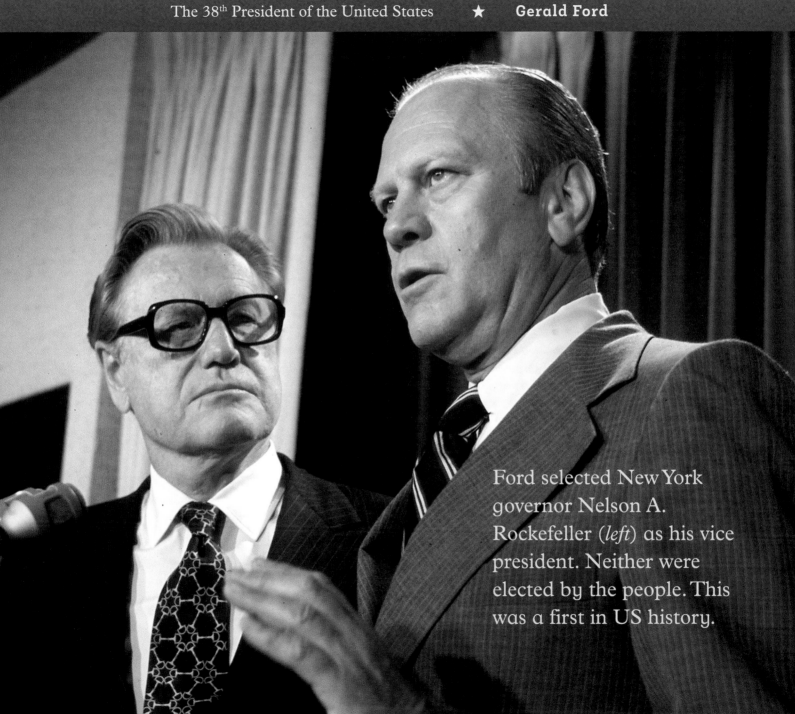

Ford selected New York governor Nelson A. Rockefeller (*left*) as his vice president. Neither were elected by the people. This was a first in US history.

President Ford

Now, Ford focused on the poor **economy**. Many people were jobless. Ford cut taxes and government spending. This created more jobs.

Meanwhile, the **Vietnam War** was ending. Ford chose to **pardon** the military deserters. This choice was not popular with many Americans.

In 1975, Ford removed the last US soldiers from Vietnam. Soon after, Cambodia captured a US ship. Ford sent US Marines to rescue the ship's crew.

SUPREME COURT APPOINTMENTS

John Paul Stevens: 1975

The country's finances slowly improved while Ford was in office.

In September 1975, Ford survived two **assassination** attempts. On September 5, Ford was in California to give a speech. There, a woman named Lynette "Squeaky" Fromme pointed a gun at him. She was caught before she could harm the president.

Seventeen days later, Ford was standing outside a California hotel. Sara Jane Moore shot at the president. Again, Ford was unhurt.

The year 1976 brought another election. On August 18, the **Republican** Party selected Ford to run for president. Ford campaigned hard. However, **Democrat** Jimmy Carter won the election.

PRESIDENT FORD'S CABINET

Ford lost the 1976 election by fewer than 2 million votes.

August 9, 1974–January 20, 1977

★ **STATE:** Henry A. Kissinger

★ **TREASURY:** William E. Simon

★ **DEFENSE:** James R. Schlesinger,
Donald Rumsfeld (from November 20, 1975)

★ **ATTORNEY GENERAL:** William B. Saxbe,
Edward H. Levi (from February 7, 1975)

★ **INTERIOR:** Rogers C.B. Morton Jr.,
Stanley K. Hathaway (from June 13, 1975),
Thomas S. Kleppe (from October 17, 1975)

★ **AGRICULTURE:** Earl L. Butz,
John A. Knebel (from November 4, 1976)

★ **COMMERCE:** Frederick B. Dent,
Rogers C.B. Morton Jr. (from May 1, 1975),
Elliot L. Richardson (from February 2, 1976)

★ **LABOR:** Peter J. Brennan,
John T. Dunlop (from March 18, 1975),
Willie J. Usery Jr. (from February 10, 1976)

★ **HEALTH, EDUCATION, AND WELFARE:**
Caspar W. Weinberger,
F. David Matthews (from August 8, 1975)

★ **HOUSING AND URBAN DEVELOPMENT:**
James T. Lynn,
Carla Anderson Hills (from March 10, 1975)

★ **TRANSPORTATION:** Claude S. Brinegar,
William T. Coleman Jr. (from March 7, 1975)

27

Retirement

Ford left the White House in January 1977. He and his family moved to Rancho Mirage, California. Ford remained active in **politics**.

In 1981, a library and a museum opened in Ford's honor. And in 1999, Ford received the Presidential Medal of Freedom. This award thanked Ford for his presidential leadership.

Gerald Ford died on December 26, 2006. Ford became vice president and president without being elected. But more importantly, he brought honor back to the White House.

President Bill Clinton and his wife, Hillary, presented
Ford with the Presidential Medal of Freedom.

Office of the President

Branches of Government

The US government has three branches. They are the executive, legislative, and judicial branches. Each branch has some power over the others. This is called a system of checks and balances.

★ Executive Branch

The executive branch enforces laws. It is made up of the president, the vice president, and the president's cabinet. The president represents the United States around the world. He or she also signs bills into law and leads the military.

★ Legislative Branch

The legislative branch makes laws, maintains the military, and regulates trade. It also has the power to declare war. This branch includes the Senate and the House of Representatives. Together, these two houses form Congress.

★ Judicial Branch

The judicial branch interprets laws. It is made up of district courts, courts of appeals, and the Supreme Court. District courts try cases. Sometimes people disagree with a trial's outcome. Then he or she may appeal. If a court of appeals supports the ruling, a person may appeal to the Supreme Court.

Qualifications for Office

To be president, a candidate must be at least 35 years old. The person must be a natural-born US citizen. He or she must also have lived in the United States for at least 14 years.

Electoral College

The US presidential election is an indirect election. Voters from each state choose electors. These electors represent their state in the Electoral College. Each elector has one electoral vote. Electors cast their vote for the candidate with the highest number of votes from people in their state. A candidate must receive the majority of Electoral College votes to win.

Term of Office

Each president may be elected to two four-year terms. The presidential election is held on the Tuesday after the first Monday in November. The president is sworn in on January 20 of the following year. At that time, he or she takes the oath of office.
It states:

> I do solemnly swear (or affirm) that I will faithfully execute the office of President of the United States, and will to the best of my ability, preserve, protect and defend the Constitution of the United States.

31

Line of Succession

The Presidential Succession Act of 1947 states who becomes president if the president cannot serve. The vice president is first in the line. Next are the Speaker of the House and the President Pro Tempore of the Senate. It may happen that none of these individuals is able to serve. Then the office falls to the president's cabinet members. They would take office in the order in which each department was created:

Secretary of State

Secretary of the Treasury

Secretary of Defense

Attorney General

Secretary of the Interior

Secretary of Agriculture

Secretary of Commerce

Secretary of Labor

Secretary of Health and Human Services

Secretary of Housing and Urban Development

Secretary of Transportation

Secretary of Energy

Secretary of Education

Secretary of Veterans Affairs

Secretary of Homeland Security

Benefits

★ While in office, the president receives a salary. It is $400,000 per year. He or she lives in the White House. The president also has 24-hour Secret Service protection.

★ The president may travel on a Boeing 747 jet. This special jet is called Air Force One. It can hold 70 passengers. It has kitchens, a dining room, sleeping areas, and more. Air Force One can fly halfway around the world before needing to refuel. It can even refuel in flight!

★ When the president travels by car, he or she uses Cadillac One. It is a Cadillac Deville that has been modified. The car has heavy armor and communications systems. The president may even take Cadillac One along when visiting other countries.

★ The president also travels on a helicopter. It is called Marine One. It may also be taken along when the president visits other countries.

★ Sometimes the president needs to get away with family and friends. Camp David is the official presidential retreat. It is located in Maryland. The US Navy maintains the retreat. The US Marine Corps keeps it secure. The camp offers swimming, tennis, golf, and hiking.

★ When the president leaves office, he or she receives lifetime Secret Service protection. He or she also receives a yearly pension of $203,700. The former president also receives money for office space, supplies, and staff.

PRESIDENTS AND THEIR TERMS

PRESIDENT	PARTY	TOOK OFFICE	LEFT OFFICE	TERMS SERVED	VICE PRESIDENT
George Washington	None	April 30, 1789	March 4, 1797	Two	John Adams
John Adams	Federalist	March 4, 1797	March 4, 1801	One	Thomas Jefferson
Thomas Jefferson	Democratic-Republican	March 4, 1801	March 4, 1809	Two	Aaron Burr, George Clinton
James Madison	Democratic-Republican	March 4, 1809	March 4, 1817	Two	George Clinton, Elbridge Gerry
James Monroe	Democratic-Republican	March 4, 1817	March 4, 1825	Two	Daniel D. Tompkins
John Quincy Adams	Democratic-Republican	March 4, 1825	March 4, 1829	One	John C. Calhoun
Andrew Jackson	Democrat	March 4, 1829	March 4, 1837	Two	John C. Calhoun, Martin Van Buren
Martin Van Buren	Democrat	March 4, 1837	March 4, 1841	One	Richard M. Johnson
William H. Harrison	Whig	March 4, 1841	April 4, 1841	Died During First Term	John Tyler
John Tyler	Whig	April 6, 1841	March 4, 1845	Completed Harrison's Term	Office Vacant
James K. Polk	Democrat	March 4, 1845	March 4, 1849	One	George M. Dallas
Zachary Taylor	Whig	March 5, 1849	July 9, 1850	Died During First Term	Millard Fillmore

PRESIDENT	PARTY	TOOK OFFICE	LEFT OFFICE	TERMS SERVED	VICE PRESIDENT
Millard Fillmore	Whig	July 10, 1850	March 4, 1853	Completed Taylor's Term	Office Vacant
Franklin Pierce	Democrat	March 4, 1853	March 4, 1857	One	William R.D. King
James Buchanan	Democrat	March 4, 1857	March 4, 1861	One	John C. Breckinridge
Abraham Lincoln	Republican	March 4, 1861	April 15, 1865	Served One Term, Died During Second Term	Hannibal Hamlin, Andrew Johnson
Andrew Johnson	Democrat	April 15, 1865	March 4, 1869	Completed Lincoln's Second Term	Office Vacant
Ulysses S. Grant	Republican	March 4, 1869	March 4, 1877	Two	Schuyler Colfax, Henry Wilson
Rutherford B. Hayes	Republican	March 3, 1877	March 4, 1881	One	William A. Wheeler
James A. Garfield	Republican	March 4, 1881	September 19, 1881	Died During First Term	Chester Arthur
Chester Arthur	Republican	September 20, 1881	March 4, 1885	Completed Garfield's Term	Office Vacant
Grover Cleveland	Democrat	March 4, 1885	March 4, 1889	One	Thomas A. Hendricks
Benjamin Harrison	Republican	March 4, 1889	March 4, 1893	One	Levi P. Morton
Grover Cleveland	Democrat	March 4, 1893	March 4, 1897	One	Adlai E. Stevenson
William McKinley	Republican	March 4, 1897	September 14, 1901	Served One Term, Died During Second Term	Garret A. Hobart, Theodore Roosevelt

PRESIDENT	PARTY	TOOK OFFICE	LEFT OFFICE	TERMS SERVED	VICE PRESIDENT
Theodore Roosevelt	Republican	September 14, 1901	March 4, 1909	Completed McKinley's Second Term, Served One Term	Office Vacant, Charles Fairbanks
William Taft	Republican	March 4, 1909	March 4, 1913	One	James S. Sherman
Woodrow Wilson	Democrat	March 4, 1913	March 4, 1921	Two	Thomas R. Marshall
Warren G. Harding	Republican	March 4, 1921	August 2, 1923	Died During First Term	Calvin Coolidge
Calvin Coolidge	Republican	August 3, 1923	March 4, 1929	Completed Harding's Term, Served One Term	Office Vacant, Charles Dawes
Herbert Hoover	Republican	March 4, 1929	March 4, 1933	One	Charles Curtis
Franklin D. Roosevelt	Democrat	March 4, 1933	April 12, 1945	Served Three Terms, Died During Fourth Term	John Nance Garner, Henry A. Wallace, Harry S. Truman
Harry S. Truman	Democrat	April 12, 1945	January 20, 1953	Completed Roosevelt's Fourth Term, Served One Term	Office Vacant, Alben Barkley
Dwight D. Eisenhower	Republican	January 20, 1953	January 20, 1961	Two	Richard Nixon
John F. Kennedy	Democrat	January 20, 1961	November 22, 1963	Died During First Term	Lyndon B. Johnson
Lyndon B. Johnson	Democrat	November 22, 1963	January 20, 1969	Completed Kennedy's Term, Served One Term	Office Vacant, Hubert H. Humphrey
Richard Nixon	Republican	January 20, 1969	August 9, 1974	Completed First Term, Resigned During Second Term	Spiro T. Agnew, Gerald Ford

PRESIDENT	PARTY	TOOK OFFICE	LEFT OFFICE	TERMS SERVED	VICE PRESIDENT
Gerald Ford	Republican	August 9, 1974	January 20, 1977	Completed Nixon's Second Term	Nelson A. Rockefeller
Jimmy Carter	Democrat	January 20, 1977	January 20, 1981	One	Walter Mondale
Ronald Reagan	Republican	January 20, 1981	January 20, 1989	Two	George H.W. Bush
George H.W. Bush	Republican	January 20, 1989	January 20, 1993	One	Dan Quayle
Bill Clinton	Democrat	January 20, 1993	January 20, 2001	Two	Al Gore
George W. Bush	Republican	January 20, 2001	January 20, 2009	Two	Dick Cheney
Barack Obama	Democrat	January 20, 2009	January 20, 2017	Two	Joe Biden

"**Freedom is always worth fighting for.**" Gerald Ford

★ WRITE TO THE PRESIDENT ★

You may write to the president at:
The White House
1600 Pennsylvania Avenue NW
Washington, DC 20500

You may e-mail the president at:
comments@whitehouse.gov

37

Glossary

assassinate—to murder an important person by a surprise or secret attack.

civil rights—the rights of a citizen, such as the right to vote or freedom of speech.

commission—a group of people who meet to solve a particular problem or do certain tasks.

Democrat—a member of the Democratic political party.

divorce—to officially end a marriage.

economy—the way that a country produces, sells, and buys goods and services. The study of producing, buying, and selling is called economics.

graduate (GRA-juh-wayt)—to complete a level of schooling.

lawyer (LAW-yuhr)—a person who gives people advice on laws or represents them in court.

lieutenant—an officer of low rank in the armed forces.

minority leader—the leader of a party that does not have the greatest number of votes in a legislative body, such as the US Senate.

pardon—to free a person from punishment for an offense.

politics—the art or science of government. Something referring to politics is political. A person who is active in politics is a politician.

representative—someone chosen in an election to act or speak for the people who voted for him or her.

Republican—a member of the Republican political party.

resign—to give up a job, position, or office by choice.

scandal—an action that shocks people and disgraces those connected with it.

support—to believe in or be in favor of something.

Vietnam War—a war that took place between South Vietnam and North Vietnam from 1957 to 1975. The United States was involved in this war for many years.

World War II—a war fought in Europe, Asia, and Africa from 1939 to 1945.

★ WEBSITES ★

To learn more about the US Presidents, visit **booklinks.abdopublishing.com**. These links are routinely monitored and updated to provide the most current information available.

Index